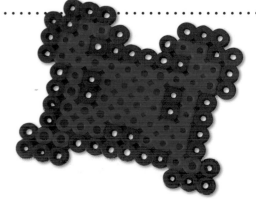

Pixelate Your Life with Fusible Beads!

Most of what we see today is made up of pixels: TVs, computer screens, smart phones, and much more. Little humble squares of color comprise everything from your alarm clock readout to a high definition movie screen. With fusible beads like those from Perler, you can unlock the power of the pixel in your own hands!

As a child I grew up in the 8-bit era of blocky video games. Though they looked simple, they had a charm that was friendly and approachable. On lazy Sunday afternoons I would copy the pixels from game magazines and the TV screen to recreate my favorite sprites on graph paper. Years later, I learned that fusible beads can be used in the same way to bring your favorite pixels into

the third dimension, creating useful objects like coasters, jewelry, toys, and other trinkets.

Crafting with fusible beads is so simple, and is perfect for creators of all ages. Combine that with the quirky and retro world of pixel art and you'll never run out of ideas. Making wonderful pixelated masterpieces is as easy as following a chart and placing beads, and when you finish you'll have a creation that looks like it stepped right out of a screen!

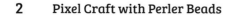

FUSIBLE BEADS

Basic beads: Basic medium-sized fusible beads, the ones used most frequently in this book, are 5mm in diameter and come in more than 50 colors. They're easy to find in local craft stores in ready-to-use kits and in a la carte bags of specific colors. The brands available include Perler, Hama, Nabbi, and Artkal. They can sometimes melt at different rates, so if you want to avoid unexpected hiccups when fusing, it's best not to mix brands.

Mini beads: Smaller versions of the basic beads are 2.5mm in diameter and are made by brands like Hama and Artkal. At half the size, they're ideal for projects with a lot of detail and a smaller result, like jewelry and pins. Mini beads require their own pegboards to fit the small size, so be sure to find those as well if you plan to try using them.

Biggie beads: Larger versions of the basic beads are 10mm in diameter and are available from Perler, Hama, and Nabbi under various names. They're best for younger children (four and up) to practice colors and motor skills, so they're not as popular as the basic size and don't come in as many colors. They also require their own specially sized board, so be sure to get that if you want to give them a try.

Special finishes: Depending on the brand, you can also find special finishes for each kind of bead, ranging from translucent, glow-in-the-dark, pearlescent, glitter, and striped finishes. They can really add a beautiful or cool touch to a project.

Basic beads. At 5mm, regular fusible beads are not too small and not too big.

QUICK START COLORS

If you're new to fusible beads and you're not sure what colors to get, your best bet is to purchase a sample tray with a bit of every color in the rainbow—these are easy to find in craft stores. Also get one or two extra packets of black and white, as they're used more often than you'd think. If you want to try specialty beads, opt for a small mixed packet, because they're not used very often in charts.

Getting Started

PEGBOARDS

Square pegboards: Your basic pegboards for regular fusible beads tend to come in a square shape that's about 5⅝" x 5⅝" (14.5 x 14.5cm) and holds a grid of 29 x 29 beads. Larger boards that go up to 10" (25.5cm) in size are also available, but a more versatile option is to get linkable boards. These boards fit together like puzzle pieces and allow you to create a space large enough to match your chart. Most of the patterns in this book use the grid pattern found on square pegboards.

Shape pegboards: Pegboards of shapes like hexagons, circles, and stars are useful because they offer something different than the usual grid layout found on square pegboards. Pegs on hexagon boards are laid out in a staggered brick pattern—every other row is shifted by one half space. Pegs on circle boards are laid out in a radial pattern, making it easy to create flawless circular designs without jagged edges. A five-point star board is also useful; its layout creates stars that look much cleaner than ones created on grid boards. Some of the patterns in this book use shape boards, so get a hexagon, a circle, and a five-point star to make all the projects.

Object and animal boards: Beyond basic shapes, bead brands offer pegboards of loads of objects and animals, too, such as flowers, cars, shoes, cats, dogs, dolphins— the list goes on. These act like color-by-numbers, allowing you to fill in the board however you like to get an expected result. However, the shapes can be limiting, and don't require separate patterns to use, so they aren't featured in this book.

EXTRAS

ADHESIVES

To make your fused bead pieces into projects other than flat, unadorned items, you'll often need adhesives.

Hot glue: Hot glue works best for adhering fused bead pieces to each other to assemble larger projects. The high-temperature glue works well because the beads react to high heat anyway. See hot glue in action while creating the 3D projects on pages 28–37.

Heavy-duty glue: This kind of glue can be used when hot glue doesn't work, such as for gluing fused bead pieces to another smooth surface. Glues for non-porous surfaces work especially well with the plastic in fusible beads. Some examples of good glues are Gorilla Glue, Liquid Fusion, and E6000.

TOOLS

Some of the tools below, like an iron and ironing paper, are essential, and others, like tweezers, just make life much easier and are worth the investment!

Iron: To fuse your beads, you'll need a nice, hot iron. You don't need anything fancy, but if you can turn off the steam function, that's a plus.

Ironing paper: Most fusible bead starter kits come with ironing paper. It protects your iron from the melting plastic while the beads fuse. It's completely reusable, but should you run out or need a bigger sheet, parchment paper from the kitchen works perfectly well, too.

Tweezers: Fusible beads are much easier to pick up and place with a trusty set of tweezers. They can be found alongside other fusible bead accessories in the craft store, but don't hesitate to try using other styles found in beauty shops, hobby shops, and hardware stores. They all have different point shapes and widths, and one might work better for you. I personally prefer to use a pair with an angled tip.

Motionators: A new product from Perler brand, Motionators hook into the holes of your bead creations to serve as hinges for boxes or movable parts for your original designs.

HOW-TO: ASSEMBLING AND FUSING BEADS

Fusing a set of beads is pretty much foolproof. Larger projects can get a bit more challenging, though, so follow the extra tips here if you run into any issues.

1 Gather your supplies. Reference your chosen pattern and assemble the bead colors necessary, the board(s) called for, your tweezers, an iron, and ironing paper. Heat up your iron to medium-high heat without steam.

2 Assemble the design. Using tweezers, assemble the beads on your board, setting each bead onto the corresponding peg following the chart. Going row by row is good for beginners; going color by color is a little harder, but much faster.

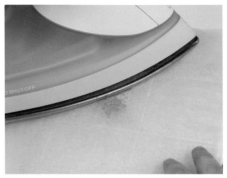

3 Iron the first side. Take your completed pegboard to a flat ironing surface. Place ironing paper over the beads. Run the hot iron in slow circles over the paper for about 5–10 seconds at a time. The beads should melt enough that you can see them sticking to the paper.

TIP

Iron the outer edges of your project first, as the beads there tend to wobble and fall over more often. Then use the tip of your iron to focus in on the center beads if they haven't melted yet.

4 Allow to cool. Let the beads cool completely (about 5–10 minutes) before continuing. For large pieces that tend to curl (or just for extra insurance), rest a few heavy books on top of the beads while they cool so the finished piece is nice and flat.

5 Iron the second side. Remove the piece from the paper and pegboard. Flip it over and place it back onto the ironing surface (you no longer need the pegboard). Rest the paper back on top of the beads and iron the piece again the same way you did in step 3. Once again, allow the piece to cool.

HOW-TO: BUILDING 3D OBJECTS

Did you know that you can create 3D objects by assembling fused bead pieces? Get tips on how to execute them flawlessly by learning how they're assembled here.

1 Assemble the design. Assemble the beads for all the pieces required to create your project. You'll see that the edges of the pieces are like puzzle pieces, with protrusions and divots. These will fit together later.

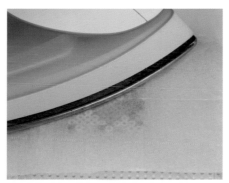

2 Iron the pieces. Iron all the pieces as in steps 3–5 of the bead fusing technique on page 6. Be sure not to iron the beads too long; you don't want them to flatten too much or they won't fit into one another. Iron them just enough to fuse them together.

3 Test the pieces. Following the project instructions, join two of the pieces together to see how they fit. If you ironed too much in step 2, just gently squeeze the pieces together to fit them into one another.

4 Join the pieces. Dab some hot glue into the nooks where the pieces join and attach them quickly. Join only a few nooks at a time and hold the pieces firmly together until the glue dries, which takes about 20–30 seconds.

5 Complete the project. Continue adding more pieces to your project as the instructions dictate, testing each join first, then using glue to secure it.

Statement Necklace

MAKES: One Necklace | Pattern on Page 10

Made from loads of small flowers, this necklace is quick to fuse up and put together. Use pearlescent beads to add a bit of shine to your finished piece—you won't believe it's made from fusible beads! The fresh color scheme will make it a real summer staple in your jewelry collection. It would look perfect with a sundress or favorite tank top on a warm day.

TOOLS

Square peg board
Hexagon peg board
Iron
Ironing paper
Jewelry pliers

BEADS

- ● 152 pearl coral
- ○ 92 pearl light pink
- ○ 112 pearl green
- ○ 94 crème
- ◎ 186 white

MATERIALS

14" (35.5cm) necklace chain with clasp

Seventeen 8mm jump rings

INSTRUCTIONS

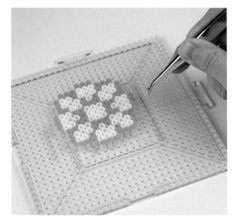

1 Assemble the beads. Following the technique on page 6, assemble and fuse the flowers following the patterns on page 10. Note that you'll need to use a hexagon board for some and a square board for others. When finished, you should have ten pieces total.

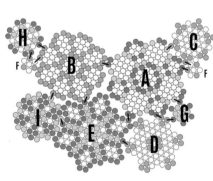

2 Arrange the flowers. Arrange the flower pieces following the illustration. Refer back to this chart as you start to join the flowers to each other in step 3.

3 Join the flowers. Starting with flower H in the upper left-hand corner, use jump rings to join each flower to the flowers beside it, following the illustration in step 2. Loop the rings through the indicated holes in the beads.

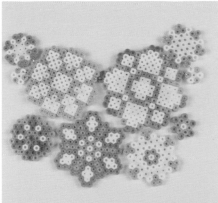

4 **Check your work.** Lay the joined flowers back down on your work surface as you go to continuously compare them to the illustration Work the top row first (shown completed in this photo), then add the pieces beneath.

5 **Add the chain.** Separate the chain into two 7" (18cm) pieces. When the flower assembly is complete, use jump rings to add one half of the chain to the upper right corner of the piece and the other half of the chain to the upper left corner.

HOW TO USE THE PATTERNS

Each pattern lists the type of pegboard you'll need and the number of beads in each color used in the design. A symbol represents the type of pegboard; check out the symbol guide at right. So, for example, if you see "■ 1", that means you need one square pegboard to make the design.

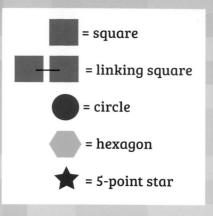

■ = square

■—■ = linking square

● = circle

⬡ = hexagon

★ = 5-point star

Statement Nacklace

■ 1, ⬡ 1

◉ 152 pearl coral

◌ 92 pearl light pink

◌ 112 pearl green

◌ 94 crème

◎ 186 white

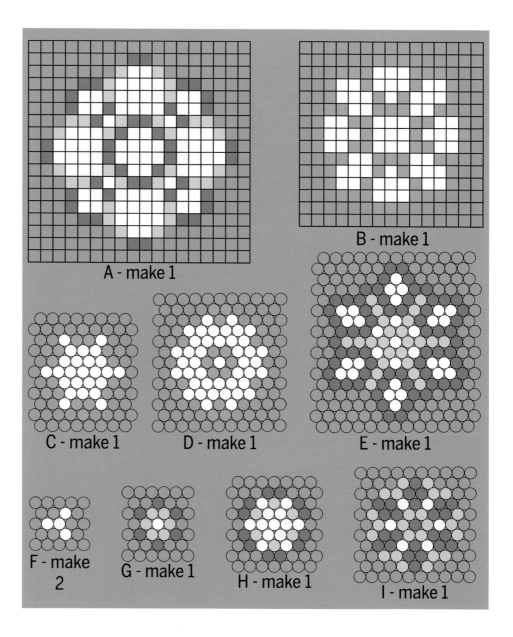

A - make 1

B - make 1

C - make 1

D - make 1

E - make 1

F - make 2

G - make 1

H - make 1

I - make 1

TINY PATTERNS

The patterns in this section measure smaller than 2" (5cm), ideal for projects like earrings, rings, charm bracelets, magnets, and more. You could also take larger patterns from this book and make them using mini beads for more tiny options.

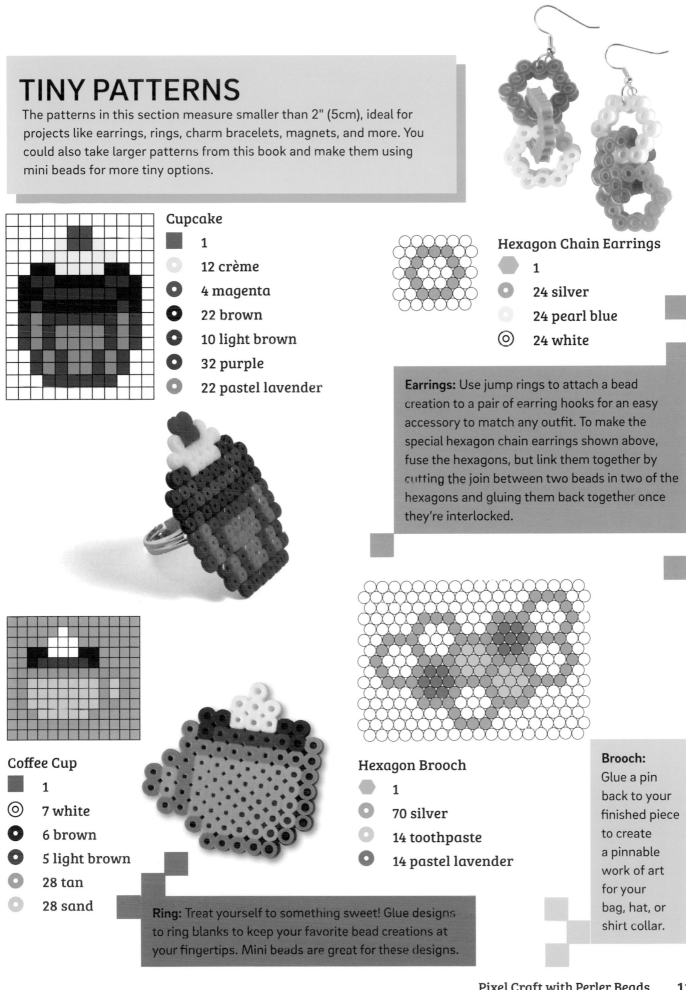

Cupcake

■	1
◯	12 crème
◉	4 magenta
◉	22 brown
◉	10 light brown
◉	32 purple
◯	22 pastel lavender

Hexagon Chain Earrings

⬡	1
◯	24 silver
◯	24 pearl blue
◎	24 white

Earrings: Use jump rings to attach a bead creation to a pair of earring hooks for an easy accessory to match any outfit. To make the special hexagon chain earrings shown above, fuse the hexagons, but link them together by cutting the join between two beads in two of the hexagons and gluing them back together once they're interlocked.

Coffee Cup

■	1
◎	7 white
⬤	6 brown
◉	5 light brown
◯	28 tan
◯	28 sand

Ring: Treat yourself to something sweet! Glue designs to ring blanks to keep your favorite bead creations at your fingertips. Mini beads are great for these designs.

Hexagon Brooch

⬡	1
◯	70 silver
◯	14 toothpaste
◯	14 pastel lavender

Brooch: Glue a pin back to your finished piece to create a pinnable work of art for your bag, hat, or shirt collar.

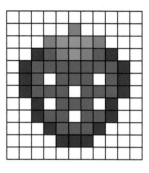

Charm Bracelet: Bring the woods with you everywhere you go with this set of five charms. Attach them to a 7" (18cm) chain using five jump rings and then add a clasp. The ones here are made with mini beads, though the tiny flower pattern on page 14 would work for regular beads.

Clover

■	1
◉	41 dark green
◉	28 pastel green
◉	24 green

Mushroom

■	1
◎	23 white
◉	36 hot coral
◉	20 red
◉	7 sand
◉	6 crème

Acorn

■	1
◉	26 dark brown
◉	13 light brown
◉	25 tan
◉	2 sand

Strawberry

■	1
◉	4 green
◉	5 dark green
◉	17 red
◉	30 hot coral
◎	6 white

Owl

■	1
◉	40 rust
◎	34 white
◉	14 tan
◉	8 cheddar
●	8 black

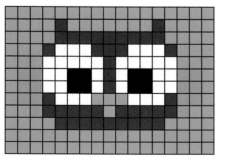

Cell Phone Charm: Latch a favorite design to a cell phone lanyard for some spot on cell phone charm. Or use it as a zipper pull for a bag or jacket so everyone can see your style from a distance.

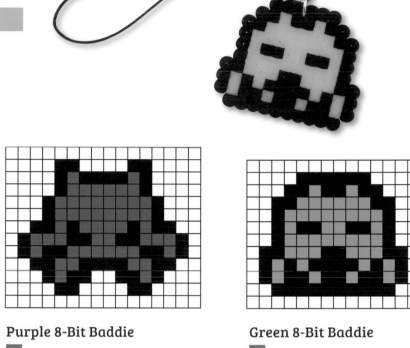

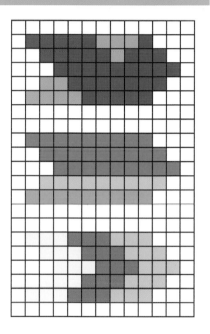

Arrowheads

■	1
	15 pastel yellow
◉	15 pastel lavender
◌	15 prickly pear
◌	9 cheddar
◌	9 toothpaste
◉	18 orange
◉	9 turquoise
◌	10 light green
◉	10 plum
◉	25 magenta

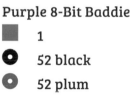

Purple 8-Bit Baddie

■	1
◉	52 black
◌	52 plum

Green 8-Bit Baddie

■	1
◉	58 black
◌	42 kiwi lime

Hair Clip: Glue a design to a sturdy hair clip for a cute accent you're sure to love. Make one in every color so you're always coordinated with your outfit!

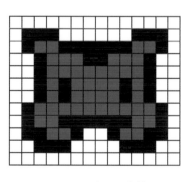

Magenta 8-Bit Baddie

■	1
◉	50 black
◌	48 magenta

Tiny Heart

■	1
◉	20 black
◌	7 magenta
◌	16 bubblegum
◌	3 light pink

Clips and Pins: Glue a small set of beads to the tip of a clothespin to brighten it up and make your office area super organized.

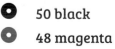

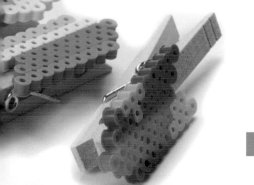

Paw Print

■		1
◎	70 clear	
●	73 black	

Tiny Flower

⬡	1	
●	6 magenta	
⬡	1 yellow	
◉	2 kiwi green	

Tiny Star

★	1	
◉	10 pastel lavender	

Push Pins: Glue particularly tiny designs to the head of a flat push pin. Add them to your trusty corkboard to completely revitalize your "To-Do" space.

OMG Word Bubble

■	1	
◎	129 white	
◉	26 gray	
●	36 black	

Heart Word Bubble

■	1	
◎	108 white	
◉	26 gray	
◉	24 bubblegum	
◉	33 light pink	

LOL! World Bubble

■	1	
◎	135 white	
◉	26 gray	
●	30 black	

Exclamation Point Word Bubble

■	1	
◎	133 white	
◉	26 gray	
●	32 black	

Magnet: Glue a strong magnet to the back of a design for a customized fridge. Use mini or regular beads for small or large versions.

14 Pixel Craft with Perler Beads

SMALL PATTERNS

These bead patterns range from 3"–5" (7.5–12.5cm) and work great for projects like headbands, keychains, and gift tags. Pick your favorites among quirky, cute, and classic designs and you'll have an army of beaded goodness when you're through.

Bow Tie: Glue a pin back to this bow tie for a quick dapper look. Pin it to your shirt collar with no complicated tying necessary!

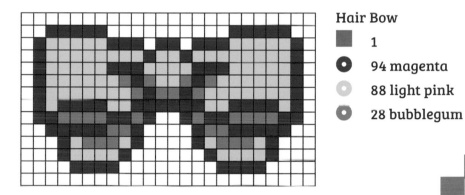

Bow Tie

 1

● 78 black

◉ 58 turquoise

◉ 42 toothpaste

◉ 8 dark blue

Hair Bow

1

● 94 magenta

◉ 88 light pink

◉ 28 bubblegum

Rose

1

● 84 red

◉ 96 black

◉ 27 cranapple

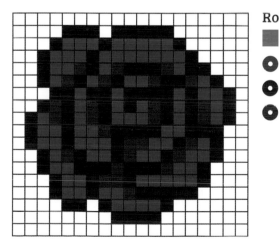

Headband: Try on your headband and mark where you'd like the beads to sit, either high on your head or more to the side. Then glue the piece in place for a darling accessory.

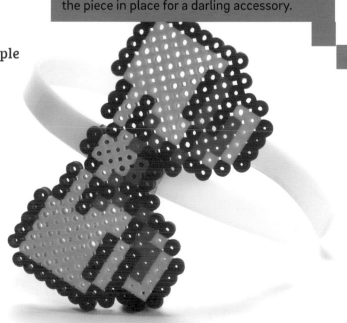

Cake Topper: Add a 4 x 8 grid of clear beads to the bottom of any bead design to turn it into a perfect cake or cupcake topper!

Candy

■	1
◉	44 parrot green
◉	48 light green
◌	20 pastel yellow
◎	32 clear

Belt Buckle: Glue two long pin backs vertically to the back of a design. Then slide it onto a thin belt as you buckle it up.

Striped Star

★	1
◉	80 silver
◎	40 white

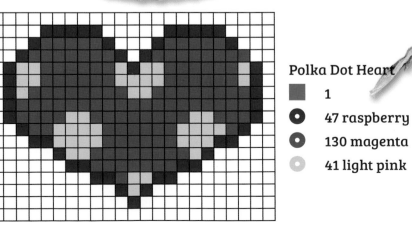

Polka Dot Heart

■	1
◉	47 raspberry
◉	130 magenta
◉	41 light pink

Gift Tag: Your next gift will be extra special with a customized gift tag. Loop a bit of ribbon through one of the beads to add that thoughtful touch. Use a yarn needle to easily thread the ribbon through tricky beads.

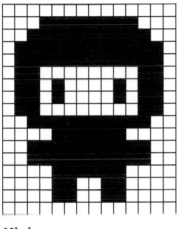

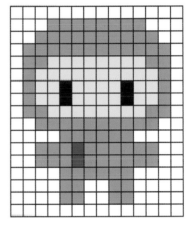

Ninja

 1

⬤ 112 black

◎ 28 white

Luchador

1

◉ 80 kiwi lime

⬤ 38 red

◎ 6 white

◉ 16 peach

Robot

1

◉ 88 gray

◉ 42 glow-in-the-dark green

⬤ 4 black

◉ 4 kiwi lime

◉ 2 magenta

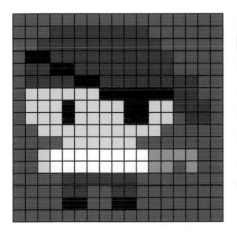

Pirate

1

◉ 63 red

◎ 16 white

⬤ 22 black

◉ 7 gray

◉ 42 peach

◉ 4 light brown

Zombie

1

◉ 86 dark green

◉ 16 light brown

◉ 8 butterscotch

⬤ 8 black

◉ 9 red

◉ 3 cranapple

◉ 10 dark blue

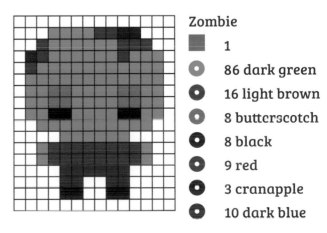

Sandals: Make a splash at the pool with these floral sandals. Attach the flowers by wrapping and gluing ribbon around the join of the flip-flop strap, then gluing the piece to the ribbon.

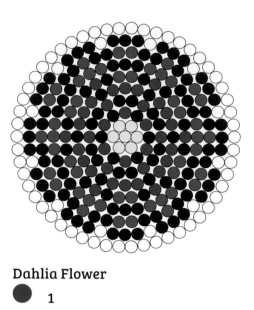

Dahlia Flower

●	1
◉	114 black
◉	48 magenta
◉	36 raspberry
◉	7 yellow

Keychain: Use jewelry pliers and a jump ring to attach a design to a keychain. Make your keychain in glow-in-the-dark beads and your keys will be easy to find in the dark!

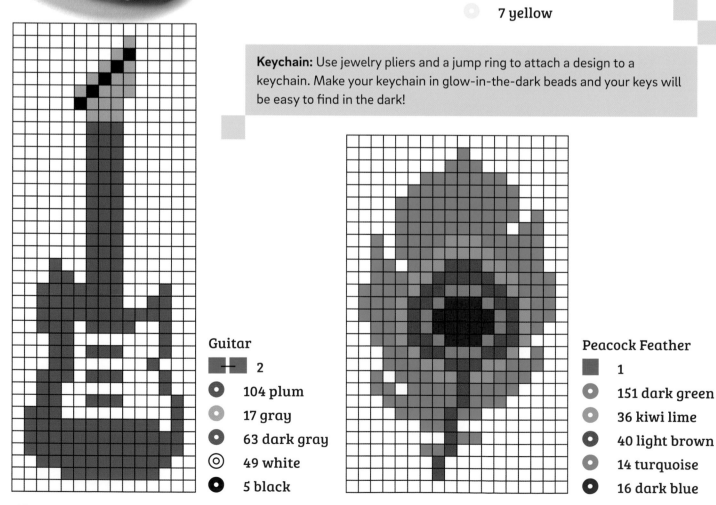

Guitar

▬ + ▬	2
◉	104 plum
◉	17 gray
◉	63 dark gray
◎	49 white
◉	5 black

Peacock Feather

■	1
◉	151 dark green
◉	36 kiwi lime
◉	40 light brown
◉	14 turquoise
◉	16 dark blue

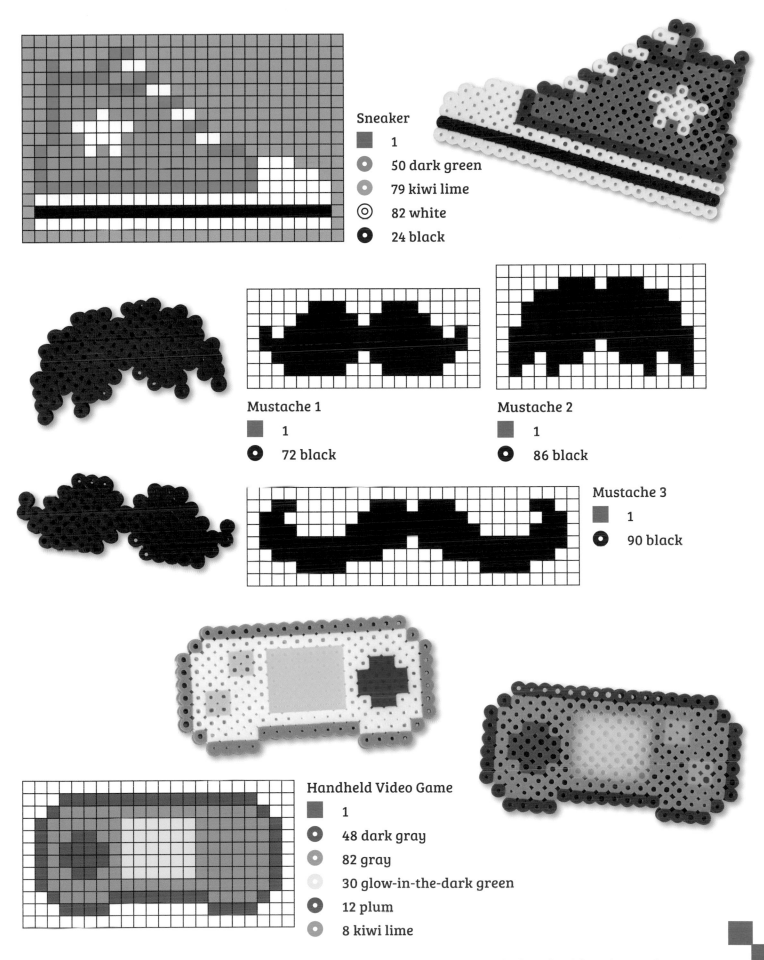

Sneaker

■	1
◉	50 dark green
◉	79 kiwi lime
◎	82 white
●	24 black

Mustache 1

■	1
●	72 black

Mustache 2

■	1
●	86 black

Mustache 3

■	1
●	90 black

Handheld Video Game

■	1
◉	48 dark gray
◉	82 gray
○	30 glow-in-the-dark green
●	12 plum
◉	8 kiwi lime

Drink Coasters

MAKES: Set of 3 coasters | Pattern on Page 22

Coasters are a classic project for fusible beads—they're easy, customizable, and oh so useful! They come together so fast, it's a cinch to make a matching set for yourself or friends, or to fuse up some to complement the season or holiday. Follow the steps here to make your own, complete with an added felt bottom to protect your tabletop and keep the coasters from sliding around.

TOOLS

Hexagon pegboard

Chalk or fabric marker

Scissors

Iron

Ironing paper

Hot glue

BEADS

Chevrons:
- 56 cheddar
- 56 orange
- 56 raspberry
- 164 crème

Triangles:
- 94 prickly pear
- 85 gray
- 86 purple
- 68 parrot green

Hexagons:
- 101 kiwi lime
- 67 bubblegum
- 67 yellow
- 97 white

MATERIALS

7" x 7" (18 x 18cm) sheet of complementary felt for each coaster

INSTRUCTIONS

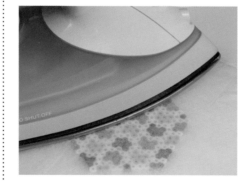

1 **Assemble the beads.** Following the technique on page 6, assemble the beaded hexagons following the patterns on page 22. Then fuse the beads on both sides as usual.

2 **Trace the felt.** Using a finished coaster, trace the shape of the hexagon onto your felt using the chalk or fabric marker.

3 **Cut the felt.** Cut out the hexagon about ¼" (0.5cm) inside the tracing you made using your scissors.

4 **Glue the felt.** Using hot glue, glue the felt to the back of your coaster, only using glue around the edges of the felt.

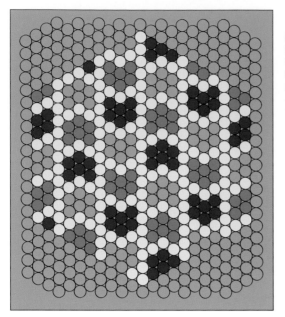

Chevrons Coaster

⬡ 1

◉ 56 cheddar

◉ 56 orange

◉ 56 raspberry

◉ 164 crème

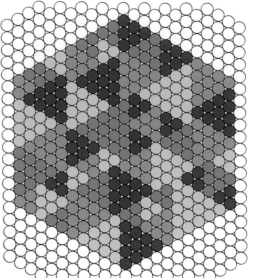

Triangles Coaster

⬡ 1

◉ 94 prickly pear

◉ 85 gray

◉ 86 purple

◉ 68 parrot green

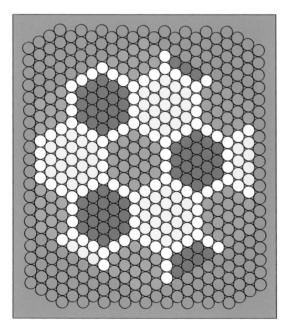

Hexagons Coaster

⬡ 1

◉ 101 kiwi lime

◉ 67 bubblegum

◉ 67 yellow

◎ 97 white

MEDIUM PATTERNS

The patterns here range from 4"–10" (10 x 25cm); they're perfect for more coasters, but can also be made into projects like drink covers, journal covers, and door hangers.

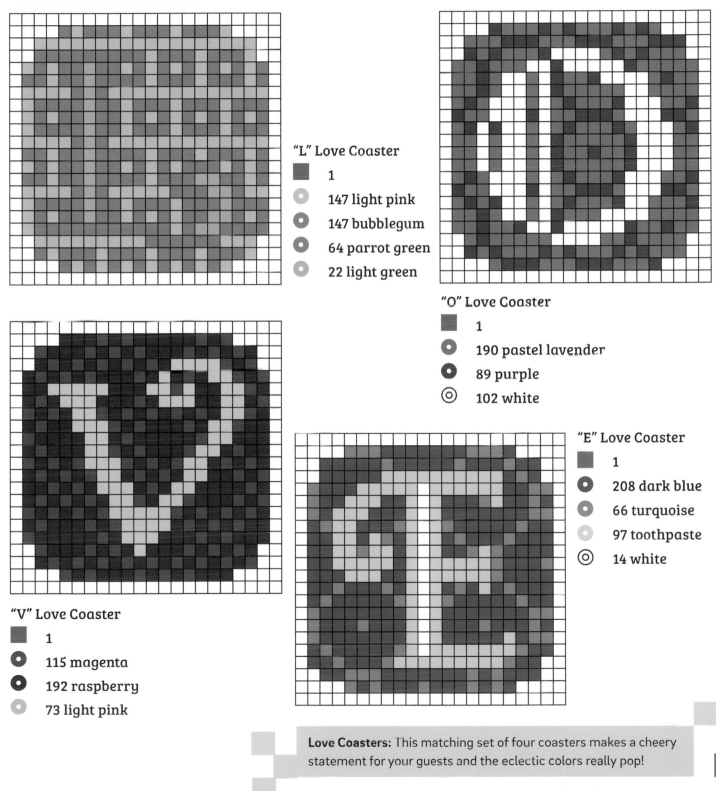

"L" Love Coaster

- ■ 1
- ⊙ 147 light pink
- ⊙ 147 bubblegum
- ⊙ 64 parrot green
- ⊙ 22 light green

"O" Love Coaster

- ■ 1
- ⊙ 190 pastel lavender
- ⊙ 89 purple
- ◎ 102 white

"E" Love Coaster

- ■ 1
- ⊙ 208 dark blue
- ⊙ 66 turquoise
- ⊙ 97 toothpaste
- ◎ 14 white

"V" Love Coaster

- ■ 1
- ⊙ 115 magenta
- ⊙ 192 raspberry
- ⊙ 73 light pink

Love Coasters: This matching set of four coasters makes a cheery statement for your guests and the eclectic colors really pop!

Stacking Tree Trunk Coasters

- 1
- 477 dark brown
- 240 light brown
- 362 tan
- 482 sand

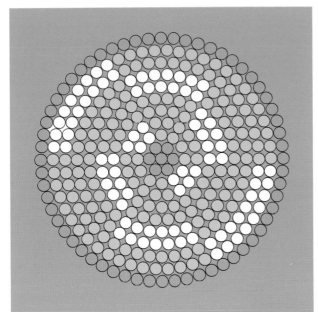

Checked Drink Cover

- ● 1
- ◎ 88 white
- ○ 88 prickly pear
- ○ 88 toothpaste

Drink Covers: These circular coasters have a hole in the center, so they can work double duty as drink covers. The hole is just large enough for your straw to fit through, so your drink will be protected from bugs during picnics and poolside lounging.

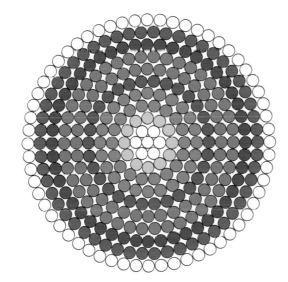

Striped Drink Cover

- ● 1
- ○ 54 plum
- ○ 48 purple
- ○ 78 pastel lavender
- ○ 30 dark blue
- ○ 42 turquoise
- ○ 12 toothpaste

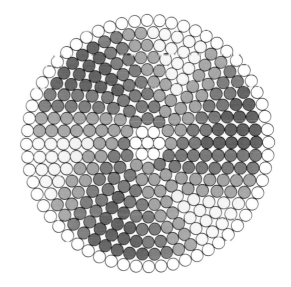

Pinwheel Drink Cover

- ● 1
- ○ 45 hot coral
- ○ 88 orange
- ○ 88 cheddar
- 45 yellow

Notebook Cover: Swap out notebook covers by unscrewing the spiral wire from a notebook, then looping the spiral through the holes of a fused bead piece. It takes a bit of patience, but the end result is a wonderful customized book that will have you itching to write.

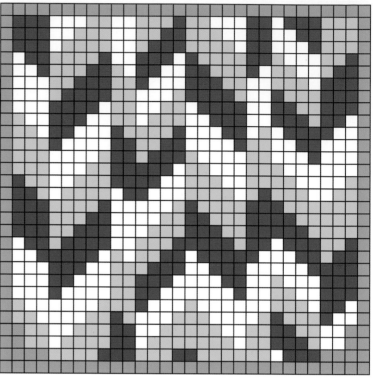

Notebook Cover

■	1
◉	267 prickly pear
◎	256 white
●	251 plum

Road Sign Door Hanger: Use this customizable door hanger to let everyone know where to find you. Thread a piece of ribbon through the holes of your beads with a yarn needle and knot each end to secure them to the hanger. Replace the sample name with yours or a friend's using the alphabet on page 27.

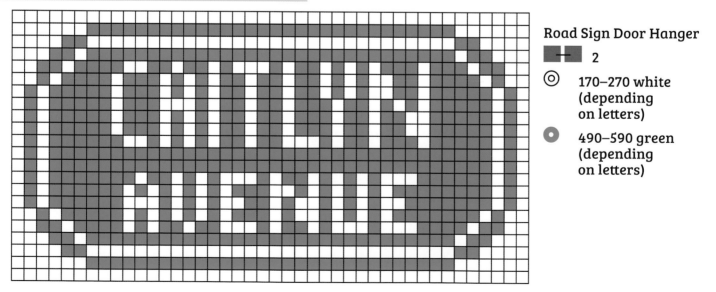

Road Sign Door Hanger

■—■	2
◎	170–270 white (depending on letters)
●	490–590 green (depending on letters)

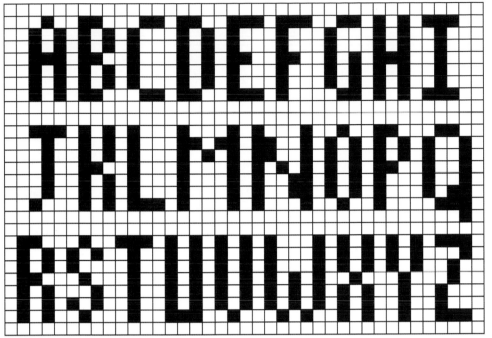

Alphabet

Use these letters to swap out the name on the door hanger with your name or a friend's, or use them in other projects.

Gift Box

MAKES: One 4" x 4" x 4" (10 x 10 x 10cm) box | Pattern on Page 30

Time to go 3D! This adorable handheld gift box will make a small present pack a big punch. It looks exactly like it's traditionally wrapped, complete with patterned paper, wide ribbon, and a tall bow. But seeing it's all made from fusible beads is sure to put a smile on the recipient's face!

BEADS

- ◯ 648 peach
- ◉ 342 blush
- ● 694 hot coral

TOOLS

Square pegboard

Iron

Ironing paper

Hot glue

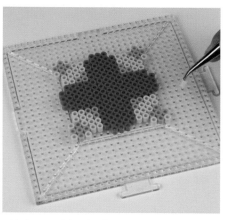

1 Assemble the beads. Using the technique on page 6, assemble and fuse the box pieces following the pattern on page 30. You should have 11 pieces total.

2 Assemble the bottom. Following the technique on page 7, assemble the bottom of the box. Start with the bottom piece and add the large side pieces around it.

3 Assemble the top. Repeat the same process as in step 2 with the top pieces: start with the largest top piece with center holes and add the short side pieces around it.

4 Add the bow. Secure the bow in the slots of the box top with a bit of glue.

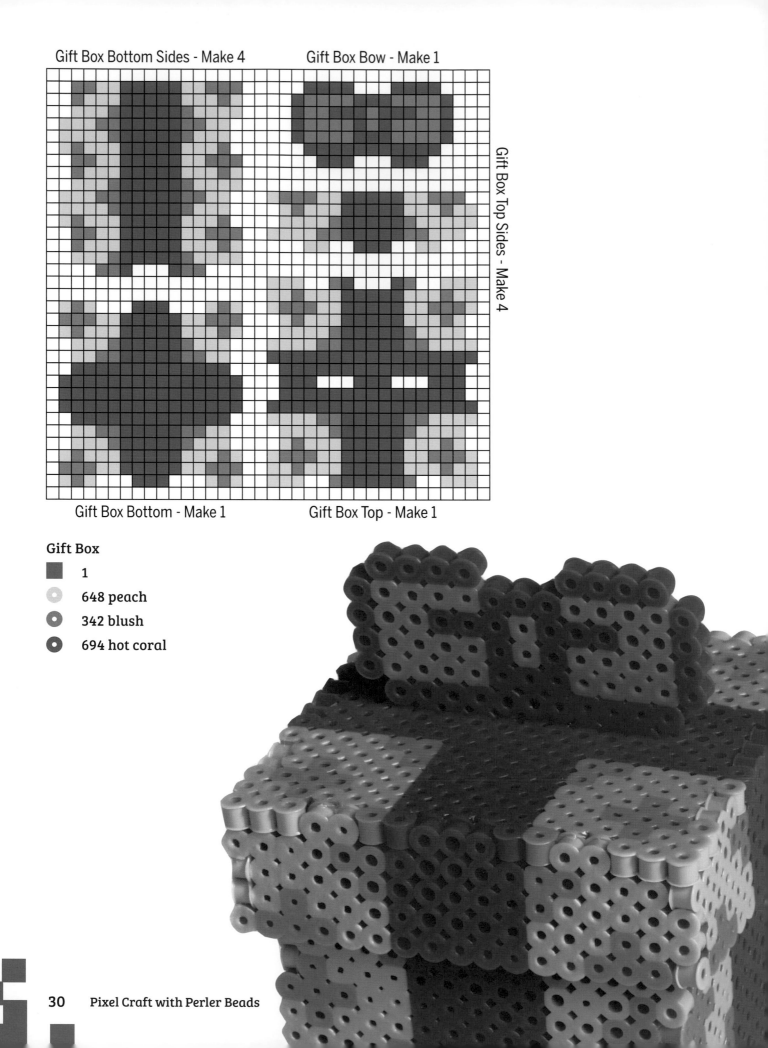

Gift Box Bottom Sides - Make 4

Gift Box Bow - Make 1

Gift Box Top Sides - Make 4

Gift Box Bottom - Make 1

Gift Box Top - Make 1

Gift Box

- 1
- 648 peach
- 342 blush
- 694 hot coral

3D PATTERNS

The projects in this section are assembled in much the same way as the gift box project. Follow the assembly diagrams to piece them together.

Planter: Make a perfect little home for your favorite cactus or other green friend. Even if you don't have a green thumb, your plant will be safe and secure.

Planter Bottom - Make 1

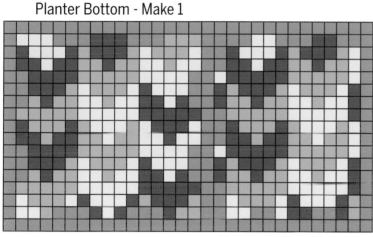

Planter Sides - Make 4

Planter

■	1
○	261 crème
◉	269 plum
○	311 pastel green

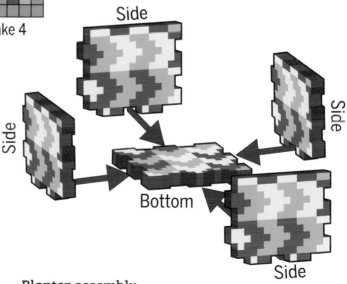

Side

Side

Side

Bottom

Side

Planter assembly

The sides fit around the bottom piece just like the gift box project, forming a box without a top.

Pencil Caddy: This useful pencil caddy holds all your most-used tools. If you love to draw or write, you'll be glad to have this at your desk.

Pencil Caddy assembly

One long side piece goes into the slots in the middle of the bottom piece, while the other two long side pieces match up with the long sides. The short front and back pieces lock into the short sides of the bottom piece.

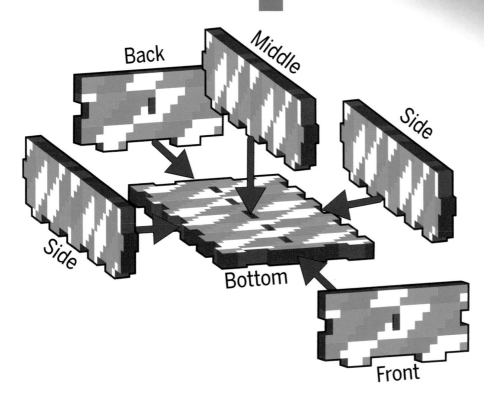

Back Middle Side Side Bottom Front

Pencil Caddy Bottom - Make 1

Pencil Caddy Sides - Make 3

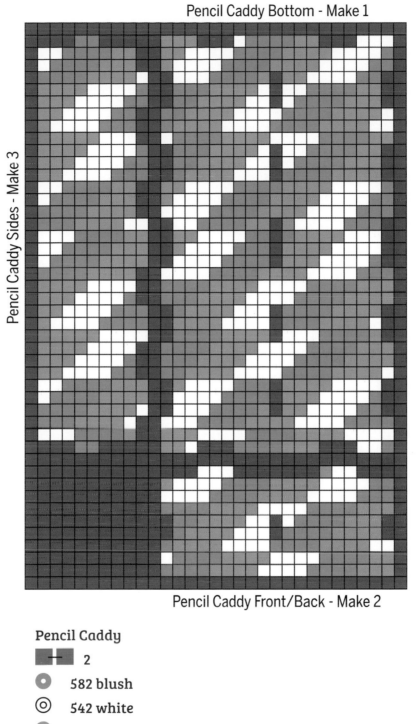

Pencil Caddy Front/Back - Make 2

Pencil Caddy

▬▬+▬	2
◉	582 blush
⊚	542 white
◉	594 gray

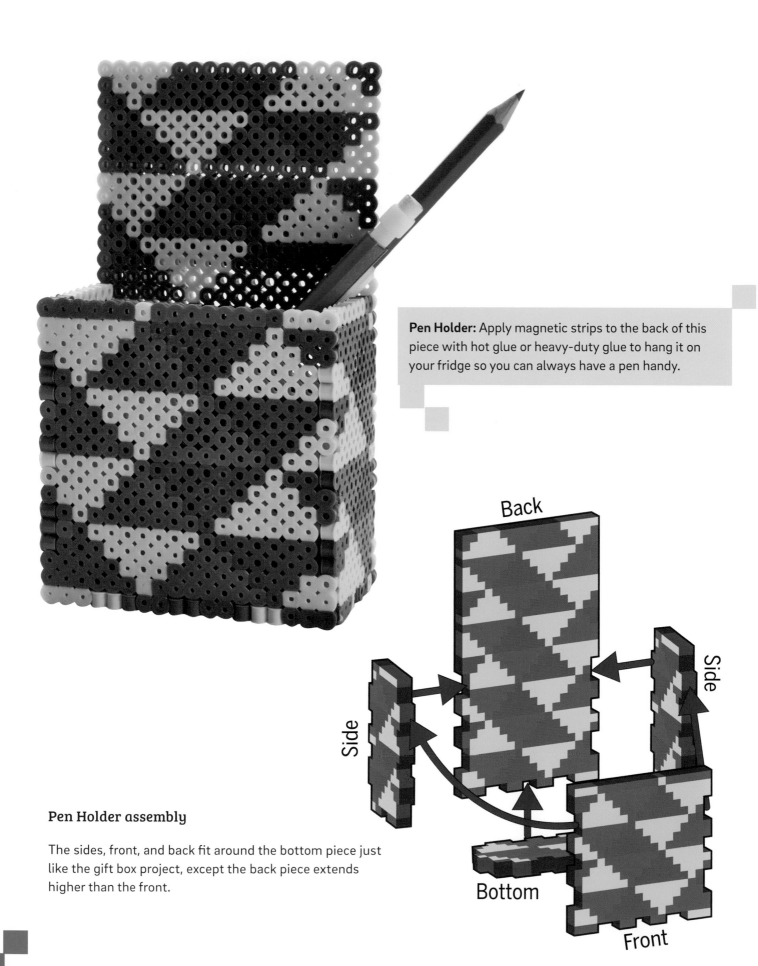

Pen Holder: Apply magnetic strips to the back of this piece with hot glue or heavy-duty glue to hang it on your fridge so you can always have a pen handy.

Back

Side

Side

Bottom

Front

Pen Holder assembly

The sides, front, and back fit around the bottom piece just like the gift box project, except the back piece extends higher than the front.

Pen Holder Back - Make 1

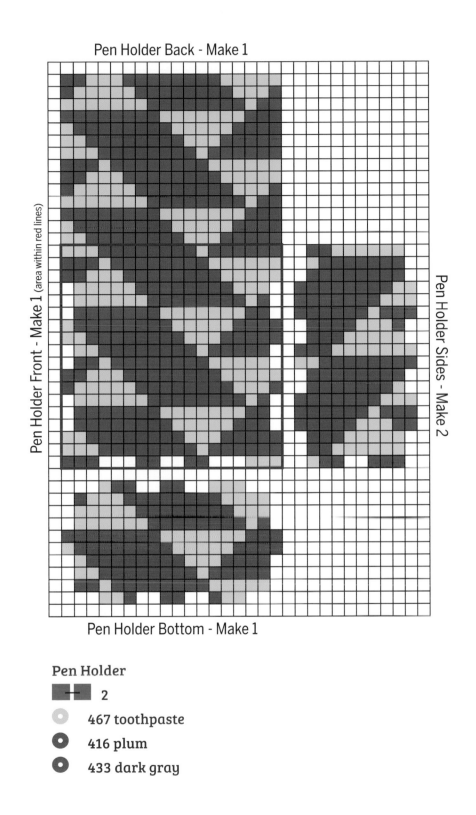

Pen Holder Front - Make 1 (area within red lines)

Pen Holder Sides - Make 2

Pen Holder Bottom - Make 1

Pen Holder

█ ┼ █ 2

◉ 467 toothpaste

◉ 416 plum

◉ 433 dark gray

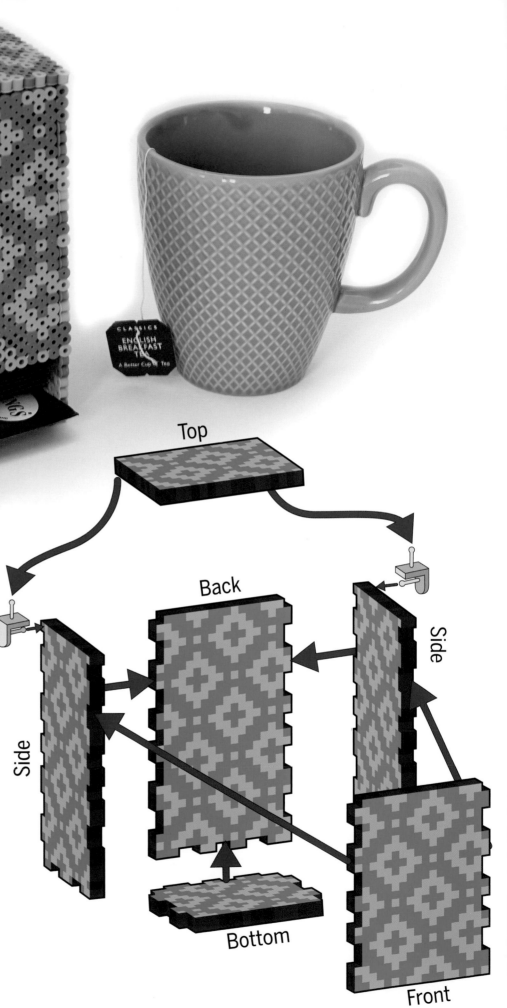

Tea Bag Dispenser: Use Motionator hinges at the top corners of this box for a flip top lid. Fill up the box and you've got a handy place to store your tea, ready to grab one bag at a time.

Tea Bag Dispenser assembly

The sides and back fit around the bottom piece like a typical box, but the front attaches flush with the top of the box, leaving a small gap at the bottom for the tea bags. The Motionators fit into the back corner bead on each side, and the top piece snaps in on top of the Motionators (it's not glued).

Top

Back

Side

Side

Bottom

Front

Tea Bag Dispenser Top - Make 1

Tea Bag Dispenser Front - Make 1 (area within red lines)

Tea Bag Dispenser Back - Make 1

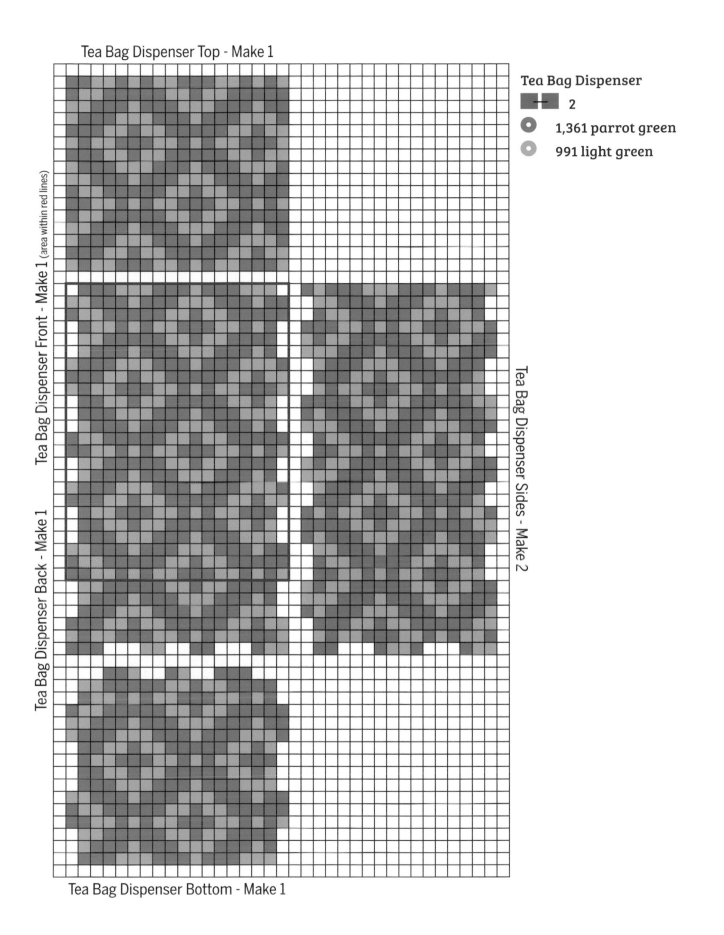

Tea Bag Dispenser

	2
⊙	1,361 parrot green
⊙	991 light green

Tea Bag Dispenser Sides - Make 2

Tea Bag Dispenser Bottom - Make 1

Bangle Bracelets

A fused strip of beads becomes a fun bangle bracelet with a glass jar and a little bit of dexterity. Finishing this project takes a bit more coordination, but once you get the hang of the fusing, you'll be able to create a whole set of colorful bracelets.

BEADS

Braid:
- 48 prickly pear
- 40 toothpaste
- 40 bubblegum

Rope:
- 48 pastel lavender
- 48 light green
- 32 gray

Zigzag:
- 88 light pink
- 132 magenta

TOOLS

Two linking square pegboards

Iron

Ironing paper

Hot glue

Glass jar about 2¼" (5.5cm) in diameter

INSTRUCTIONS

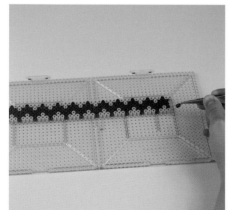

1 **Assemble the beads.** Following the technique on page 6, assemble a bead bracelet pattern from pages 40–41. Fuse only one side of the beads.

2 **Join the ends.** Bring the ends of the bracelet together with the unfused beads facing outward. Glue the ends together with hot glue to hold the bracelet in place.

3 **Fuse the front.** Slide the glued bracelet onto the jar and fuse the unfused side (facing out) with your iron. Press the bracelet against the jar carefully, fusing a few inches at a time and then rotating it.

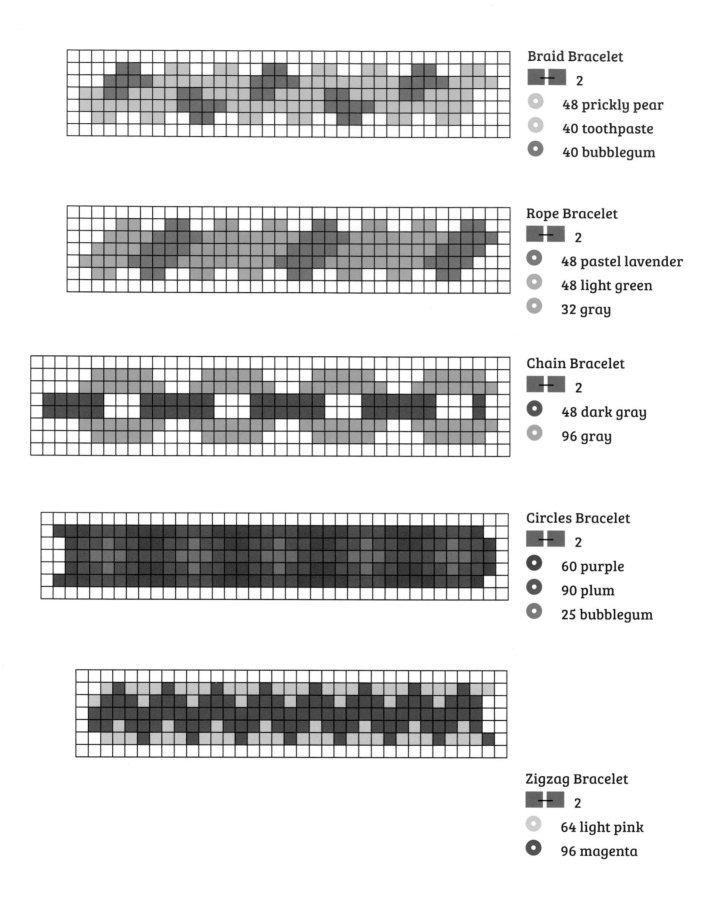

Braid Bracelet

■—■ 2

⊙ 48 prickly pear
⊙ 40 toothpaste
⊙ 40 bubblegum

Rope Bracelet

■■ 2

⊙ 48 pastel lavender
⊙ 48 light green
⊙ 32 gray

Chain Bracelet

■—■ 2

⊙ 48 dark gray
⊙ 96 gray

Circles Bracelet

■—■ 2

⊙ 60 purple
⊙ 90 plum
⊙ 25 bubblegum

Zigzag Bracelet

■—■ 2

⊙ 64 light pink
⊙ 96 magenta

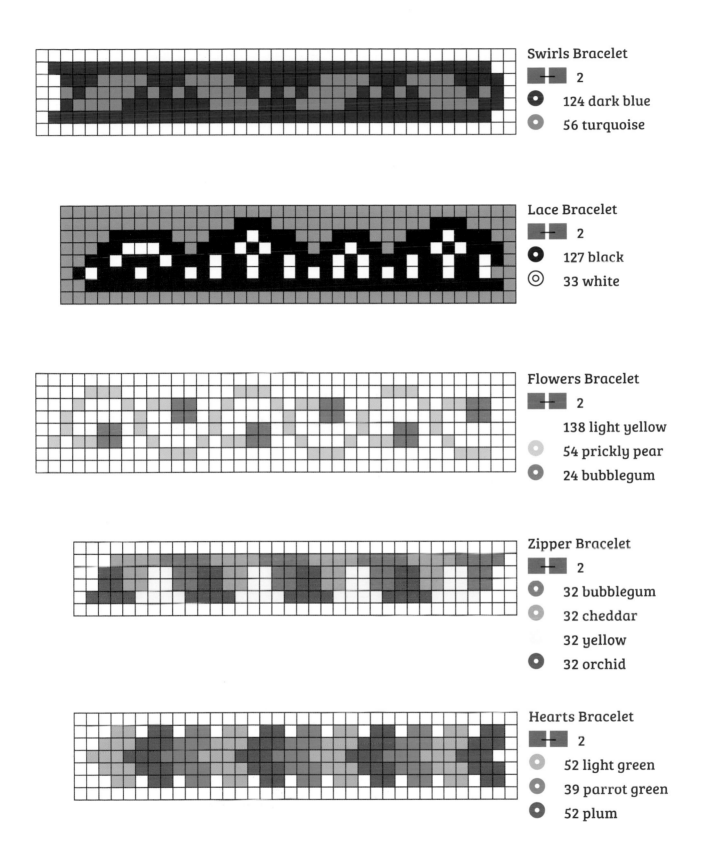

Swirls Bracelet

⬛➡⬛ 2

◉ 124 dark blue

◉ 56 turquoise

Lace Bracelet

⬛➡⬛ 2

◉ 127 black

◎ 33 white

Flowers Bracelet

⬛➡⬛ 2

138 light yellow

◉ 54 prickly pear

◉ 24 bubblegum

Zipper Bracelet

⬛➡⬛ 2

◉ 32 bubblegum

◉ 32 cheddar

32 yellow

◉ 32 orchid

Hearts Bracelet

⬛➡⬛ 2

◉ 52 light green

◉ 39 parrot green

◉ 52 plum

Picture Frames

MAKES: One 7" x 5" (18 x 12.5cm) rectangular frame (holds a 6" x 4" [15 x 10cm] photo) or one 5" x 5½" (12.5 x 14cm) hexagonal frame (holds a 4" x 4½" [10 x 11.5cm] photo) | Pattern on Pages 44–45

Keep cherished memories with you forever using these fun decorative frames. Swap out the colors so they match those in the photo, or even change the dimensions of the pattern so the frame fits your picture perfectly. No matter what, your finished project will make your photo look as bright and cheery as the memories it holds.

TOOLS

Hexagon: hexagon pegboard

Rectangle: two linking square and one hexagon pegboards

Iron

Ironing paper

Hot glue

Tape

BEADS

Hexagon:

138 light yellow

138 light green

160 prickly pear

Rectangle:

160 blueberry cream

200 plum

170 dark gray

MATERIALS

Hexagon: 5" x 5" (12.5 x 12.5cm) square of cardboard

Rectangle: 7" x 5" (18 x 12.5cm) piece of cardboard

Photo

INSTRUCTIONS

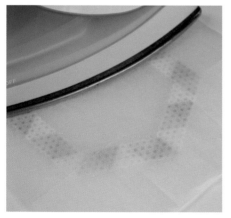

1 Assemble the beads. Following the technique on page 6, assemble and fuse the beads from one of the patterns on pages 44–45.

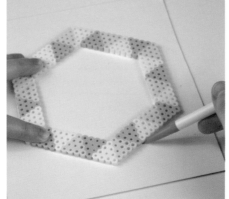

2 Trace the cardboard. Use the outside of the frame to trace the frame shape on a piece of cardboard. Also trace the inner opening of the frame on the back side of the photo.

3 Cut the cardboard. Cut out the cardboard about ¼" (5mm) inside the traced line. Cut out the photo about ¼" (5mm) outside the traced line.

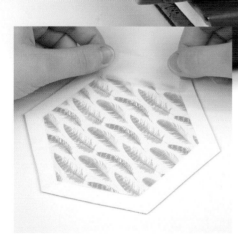

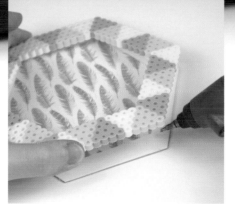

4 **Tape the photo.** Center the photo on the cardboard backing, right side facing up. Tape the edge of the photo to the cardboard, keeping the tape as close to the edges as possible.

5 **Glue the back.** Lay the frame down over the photo. Glue the frame in place along the edges.

6 **Glue the stand.** Glue the stand to the back of the frame with the bottom point of the triangle flush with the bottom of the frame, so that the frame sits on a flat surface with an upward tilt.

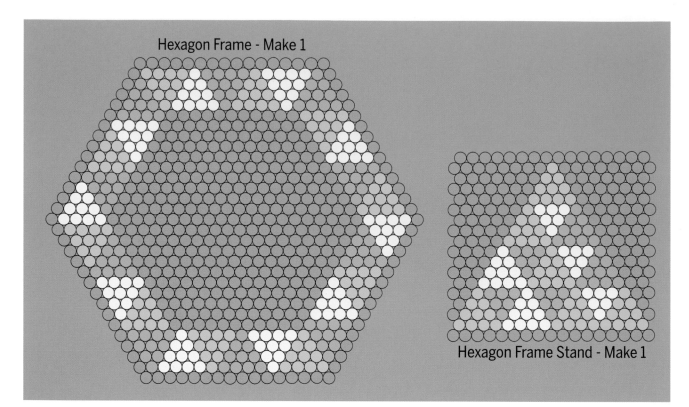

Hexagon Frame - Make 1

Hexagon Frame Stand - Make 1

Hexagon Frame

⬡ 1

○ 138 light yellow

◉ 138 light green

◉ 160 prickly pear

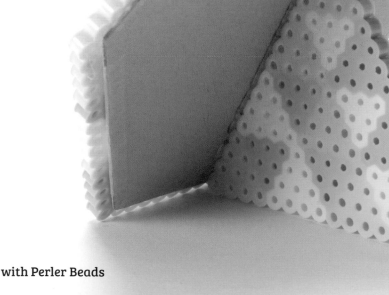

Rectangle Frame - Make 1

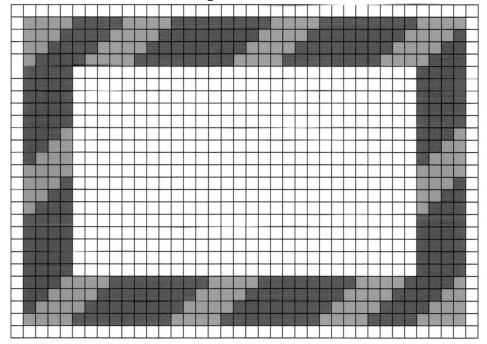

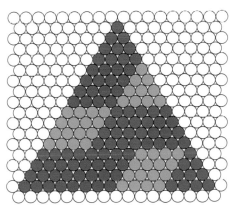

Rectangle Frame Stand - Make 1

Rectangle Frame

 1, ▬▬ 2

◎ 160 blueberry cream

◉ 200 plum

◉ 170 dark gray

Jewelry Tree

MAKES: One 6½" x 7" (16.5 x 18cm) tree | Pattern on Page 48

This decorative 3D cherry blossom tree will make your room feel like spring all year round. Use the lower branches to hang hook earrings, the upper branches to rest your rings, and all the beads in between to hook your post earrings. Even if you don't need it for jewelry, it will still brighten up any space.

BEADS

- ○ 276 light pink
- ◓ 64 bubblegum
- ◉ 588 light brown
- ● 199 brown

TOOLS

Four linking square pegboards
Iron
Ironing paper
Hot glue

INSTRUCTIONS

1 **Assemble the beads.** Following the technique on page 6, assemble and fuse the beads from the chart on page 48.

2 **Assemble the pieces.** Slide the top piece over the center of the base piece, matching the notches. When assembled correctly, the bottom edges should be flush with each other.

3 **Glue the pieces.** When you've assembled the pieces as you like, go back and add dabs of hot glue to the center notches for insurance and to keep the sides standing tall and straight.

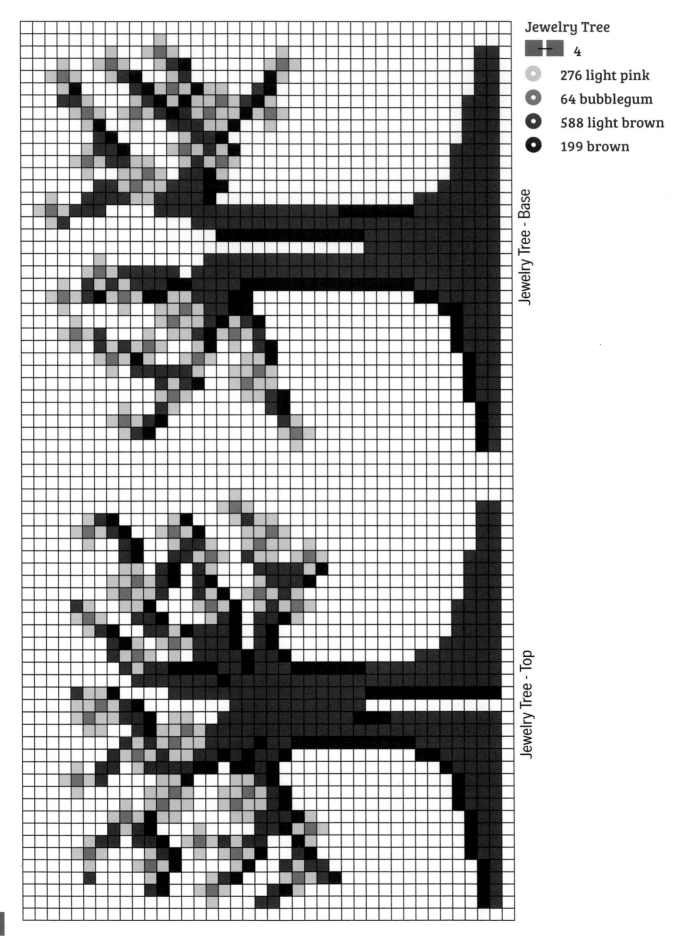

4

276 light pink

64 bubblegum

588 light brown

199 brown

Jewelry Tree - Base

Jewelry Tree - Top